MW00964205

Inspired
EMOTIONS

Written by
AMY ROBINSON

Copyright © 2015 by Amy Robinson. 727754
Library of Congress Control Number: 2015918387

ISBN: Softcover   978-1-5144-2371-4
        Hardcover   978-1-5144-2372-1
        EBook   978-1-5144-2370-7

All rights reserved. No part of this book may be reproduced
or transmitted in any form or by any means, electronic or
mechanical, including photocopying, recording, or by any
information storage and retrieval system, without permission
in writing from the copyright owner.

This is a work of fiction. Names, characters, places and
incidents either are the product of the author's imagination
or are used fictitiously, and any resemblance to any actual
persons, living or dead, events, or locales is entirely
coincidental.

Printed in Canada

Rev. date: 01/26/2015

To order additional copies of this book, contact:
Xlibris
1-888-795-4274
www.Xlibris.com
Orders@Xlibris.com

Inspired Emotions

Keeping Secrets

Keeping secrets is one thing that nobody should bear,
People only make it a secret if they know someone will care.

Sometimes the secret comes from those we've grown to love and trust,
But it's time we learn to speak up now, telling is a must.

They may say things to make you scared or have feelings of pure guilt,
But do not fall for it all, it's a big lie that they've built.

Even if they threaten you; not to say a thing,
Or try to buy your quietness with a little bit of bling.

You know, you know the difference of feeling right from wrong,
I know it can be hard to do but we have to be real strong.

Letting someone know your secret, if you have one right away,
Not only will make you feel better, but could save a life one day.

You should never keep a secret that makes you feel bad
Tell someone you look up to; a teacher, Mom or Dad.

Dreams Without Limits

Sitting in the park one day; my butt planted on the ground,
Seeing birds searching for food and soaring all around.

Looking up into the sky I see an airplane flying by,
Not knowing how it stays up there I eagerly wonder why?

Why is it that we can soar 10,000 feet above?
It must be something magical or is it determination and love?

Flying like a beautiful bird is a passion that many have had;
Turning your passion into reality can never turn out bad.

If we want to do something like build and fly a plane,
Our hands and hearts must work together as well as our brain.

We have to sit and figure out exactly what we to do,
Being very open and patient helps ideas come to you.

There will always be some obstacles that we will have to face,
But if we never ever tried; would we have ever made it into space?

Obstacles come in many forms some good some bad some scary,
The time it takes us to break through them will likely always vary.

Looking at that plane again, now seeing someone's dream;
It shows me that there are no limits no matter how unlikely they may seem.

In a Hurry Going Nowhere

I was in a hurry going nowhere; it got me to this place,
I wish I told myself back then that life is not a race.

I was racing to the convenience store with nothing else to do;
I raced so fast; if cars had wings I'm sure it would have flew.

I was pushy in the lineup and acted like a jerk,
The lady behind the counter was only doing her work.

I never said please or thank you or even looked her in the eyes;
I was in a hurry going nowhere and snickered as she sighed.

Peeling out of the driveway smoke all in the air;
Screeching tires below me, people turned to stare.

I hauled out to the stoplight just as it turned red;
I thought I could make it really fast, who knew I'd end up dead.

I floated from my body and watched down from above,
Wondering what just happened then the big guy said with love.

"You were in a hurry going nowhere, no one told you to slow down,
To stop and enjoy the simple things that life always brings around.

The Kindness of the people, that we meet and greet each day;
Maybe we can change a life with what we do and say"

I was in a hurry going nowhere and now that I am gone,
I can see the things I should have done and where I had gone wrong.

If I could turn the clock back to earlier that day,
I would have done so many things in a different way.

Kindness goes a long way, with everything we do;
Bringing it to someone's life can make you happy too.

Strong and Free

Canada is a basic term for the Country we call home,
So many different cultures here; no one stands alone.

We stand up for our freedom, for what is right and what is wrong;
Uniting with one another to keep our country strong.

We have some common rules to follow to keep us all in order,
The rules change a little bit as we go across the border.

Like ages we're allowed to vote, or learn to drive a car,
Or when we are a legal age to drink inside a bar.

Province to province, place to place small rules may be changed,
But overall these rules to our whole country still remain.

We're not allowed to steal or fight, or take somebodies life,
We're not allowed to drink and drive or sleep with anyone's Wife.

These rules keep us feeling safe, living day to day,
Breaking these simple rules, a hefty price to pay.

Freedom is what we all strive for, Canadian or not,
Religion is a way to get there, naturally we're taught.

Religion has the power to tear our country apart,
But why not love our fellow Canadians with an open loving heart?

With all the different religions, here's one main common ground,
The praise of a much higher power; that's not physically around.

Some may call it Energy, The Source, or Mighty Spirit;
It should not matter who it is or how we choose to hear it.

Others call it Buddha, Karma, Quran or God,
Whichever one you're connected to will leave you feeling Awed.

The Awe-ness that you're feeling brings power to your soul,
The feeling is contagious and helps our country as a whole.

Combining all that power is how our country came to be,
Living all together here, "True North Strong and Free".

One more little thing that we are happy to be able to say,
We are proud to be Canadian each and every day.

Meeting of Fate

I once met a girl who was only just seven;
She said she talked with those in Heaven.

She said that every single day,
The spirits always came her way.

When she told me I looked right down,
I thought she was just fooling around.

I was scared to look her in the eyes;
I did not want to get caught in her lies.

It was safe to say, I was not very sure;
I sat there really just to please her.

She opened her mouth and the words that she said,
Shivered up my spine and went into my head.

For every word she said was so true,
She even knew I just got over the flu.

She told me things that she should have never known,
Like the pet names my Grandma used on the phone.

My Grandma died when I was seven,
I knew that she had gone to Heaven.

I did not know Heaven was so close,
Seen by some but ignored by most.

I thanked her she really made my day,
And then she got up and walked away.

I now realize that Heaven is near,
She made that very, very clear.

I never forgot a word that she said;
It still floats around inside of my head.

I now talk to my Grandma every night,
Right before I turn out my light.

I know she hears every word that I say;
She sends sweet messages over my way.

I know now that life still goes on,
even when our bodies are gone.

The little girl I met that day;
Had changed my life in so many ways.

Message from Above

If fear is all that's holding you still,
Please realize your own free will.

It's ok for you to let go,
I'm happy, I'm safe and I want you to know.

I will see to it that your needs are met,
Don't worry about a thing my pet.

The love between us will never die,
I will always be watching from the sky.

I hear you when you talk to me,
The sound of your voice so gracefully.

Please know it's now time for you to move on,
The physical relationship we had is now gone.

You will always have me in your mind,
But this man that I sent you is a one of a kind.

The words he whispers are so true,
He really will take great care of you.

I send this with my heart so wide;
We will meet again on the other side.

My Hero

I had a really bad dream while sleeping late last night,
It made me cry out to my Mom and gave me quite the fright.

I dreamt about the Boogie Man; waiting there for me,
He was asking me all kinds of things; he wouldn't leave me be.

He asked me about my Mom and Dad; my Sister and Brother too,
I felt so panicked in my dreams; I didn't know what to do.

Well I stood up to the Boogie Man; and told him to leave me alone,
I told him he's not welcome here and had to leave our home.

The Boogie Man had heard me yell and now he's red hot mad,
I was really scared that in my dreams, things were about to go bad.

The Boogie Man then grabbed me; and held me in the air,
Even though it was a dream it gave me quite the scare.

I will never forget the moment; when my grandpa rescued me,
In the air still screaming there; his face I sure did see.

His words they came so clearly; he told me to hold on,
Together we flew to a magical place; where the Boogie Man was gone.

I told Grandpa I miss him; and I think of him every day,
I know now that he's here with me every step of the way.

Grandpa then had told me that I don't have to sleep in fear,
He told me if I open my eyes my bad dreams will disappear.

I did just what my Grandpa said; I wished I never though,
For when I opened my big brown eyes my Grandpa had to go.

I woke up with so many tears rolling down my face,
My Grandpa will always be my hero; he'll never be replaced.

Saying Goodbye

Sitting in this hospital bed; life now quickly passing by,
Knowing that I won't come out; here's where I'm supposed to die.

Saying goodbye to my Wife, my Children and Grandchildren too,
Is something I'm afraid of but is something that I must do.

I'll never understand exactly where I'll go,
Only God knows of that and soon to me he'll show.

I've lost so many loves one through my many years,
Knowing I will see them soon really fades my fears.

Soon I'll be an angel watching from the sky,
Protecting all my loved ones and greeting them when they die.

The memories that we shared together is something you'll always keep,
But now it's time to close my eyes and drift off into sleep.

Never Underestimate

Sitting outside the grocery store in my Mommy's car;
Being in the backseat, all the buttons were too far.

Buckled in my car seat, it was starting to get hot,
Wishing Momma would hurry up; she's all I really got.

Crying in the backseat, Mommy's taking way to long.
How would she ever know if something had gone wrong?

Beads of sweat dripped off my face; there was nothing I could do,
Buckled in my car seat, I was stuck to it like glue.

I finally stopped my crying and started to pass out;
I know my Mommy loves me; I'm all she talks about.

Mommy finally came out; I gave her quite the scare;
She pulled me out of the car seat and dumped water in my hair.

The water did me wonders; it cooled me right down;
Mommy learned a lesson that day, that she now shares around;

"Never underestimate what a few minutes can do,
It's not hard to unbuckle them and bring them In with you.

Our babies are so dear to us just what we've always wanted;
If something ever happened to them our lives would sure be haunted.

So take the time, unbuckle them and bring them in with you,
I know it's sometimes tough on you but you'll feel better if you do."

Sitting in the shopping cart, now heading into the store;
Great big grin upon my face, excited to explore.

Treasured Memories

My Grandma was my very best friend,
She loved to dance and play pretend.

We'd laugh and sing our silly ways;
She always knew how to make my day.

Three days a week she came to see me;
On those days I was so lucky to be me.

I loved my Grandma's great big heart;
Our love could never be torn apart.

Grandma once looked me in the eyes,
She told me to never tell a lie.

Then she told me she was sick,
I thought it was just a nasty trick.

The two of us went out together,
Even in the stormy weather.

Together we planted an apple tree,
In sake of Grandmas' memory.

She told me that whenever I cried,
I could talk to her up in the sky.

I realized then that she was not lying;
My Grandma really was actually dying.

We really did not have to long,
Before we sang our very last song.

I seen my Grandma in her bed,
I placed a kiss upon her head.

I stood there trying not to cry,
I hate having to say goodbye.

I placed some flowers above your grave;
I promised you I would be very brave.

Every time I see our tree,
You're always in my memory.

My Grandma was my very best friend;
I will love her till my very end.

Karma

Walking through the gravel pit with a crescent wrench in hand,
Heading to fix the screener so it could continue making sand.

I seen an agate on the ground just glowing in the sun,
The excitement that I felt right then; too it I had to run.

As I picked the agate up and held it in the air;
I notice not far from me was a big old Momma bear.

She frightened me, my heart had stopped; then started beating really fast,
This moment in my head seemed to last and last and last.

I looked at her, she looked at me then started over my way;
I quickly asked myself the question "Should I run or should I stay?"

As quickly as I thought it through, it was already to late;
The bear was standing right beside me .. I prayed for my good fate.

The bear had hovered way above me, standing on two feet.
I thought I was going to die just then, my ancestors I'd soon meet.

Then she kind of nudged me, a little with her paw;
She showed me that her paw was hurt, it was bloody and quite raw.

I seen a twig jammed in her foot that she really needed out,
When I yanked the twig on out and big roar she did shout.

I closed my eyes and braced myself now getting ready to die,
When nothing happened for minutes I slowly opened an eye.

Seeing her in a distance walking away from me,
I started laughing to myself how lucky could I be.

Karma plays a big, huge role in every day we live,
So if you want live with luck, good karma you should give.

I walked on to the screener and tightened the loose belt,
Couldn't help but smile large; so may emotions to be felt.

Even though no one will believe me, I'll tell you all today.
An angel had me help the bear and saved me from harm's way.

No Fear

Why is it we all let fear try to run our life?
The pain we achieve from the fear cuts deeper than a knife.

Bringing only stress and tears and feelings of pure hate,
If only one can change the fear before it is to late

How can one change it; I really do not know,
But something has to change real soon so life can continue to flow.

Maybe if one turns the fear into love and trust,
And really feel it deep inside, believing is a must.

Making bright new moments with every positive thought,
Can't for see the outcome, but it's all ones really got.

My Grandpa

My Grandpa is my favorite old guy;
He teaches me to always reach for the sky.

He says "It does not matter what you do,
For I will always, always love you."

I look up into my Grandpas eyes,
Knowing that he tells no lies.

He tells me that when my Dad was young,
He was always finding new ways to have fun.

He caught Snakes, Frogs and Squirrels
Which made Grandmas toes just curl.

But when he caught the great big spider,
Grandma turned into a fighter.

Grandpa said Dad laughed with glee,
It almost made him have to flee.

Grandpa still likes a good laugh now and then,
Being with me makes him feel like he's ten.

My Grandpa always looks at my hands,
And says I will turn into a strong man.

He says I look just like my Dad,
For that he is extremely glad.

For my Dad was his only boy
And brought my Grandpas heart such joy.

My Dad died when I was three,
He died fighting for our Country.

Grandpa says that when you die,
You go to Heaven up in the sky.

He says Dad hears every word that I say,
And if I wanted I could talk to him every single day.

Grandpas stories all end with a sigh,
For its all he can do to keep my Dad's memory alive.

My Dad is often on my mind,
But my Grandpa, now he's a one of a kind.

xoxo

Amy May ♡